ANIMAL RECORD BREAKERS

OSTRICH

THE LARGEST BIRD

THERESA EMMINIZER

PowerKiDS press
New York

Published in 2020 by The Rosen Publishing Group, Inc.
29 East 21st Street, New York, NY 10010

First Edition

Editor: Theresa Emminizer
Book Design: Reann Nye

Photo Credits: Series art (frame) HiSunnySky/Shutterstock.com; series art (banner) Roberto Castillo/Shutterstock.com; series art (background) Wilqkuku/Shutterstock.com; cover Radek Borovka/Shutterstock.com; p. 5 Merrillie Redden/Shutterstock.com; p. 7 (Rhea) pandapaw/Shutterstock.com; p. 7 (kiwi) Eric Isselee/Shutterstock.com; p. 7 (cassowary) Sanit Fuangnakhon/Shutterstock.com; p. 7 (emu) photomaster/Shutterstock.com; p. 9 Dirk M. de Boer/Shutterstock.com; p. 11 Dominique de La Croix/Shutterstock.com; p. 13 Stephanie Periquet/Shutterstock.com; p. 15 Andrzej Kubik/Shutterstock.com; p. 17 SKphotographer/Shutterstock.com; p. 19 talseN/Shutterstock.com; p. 21 Sergei25/Shutterstock.com; p. 22 Aaron Amat/Shutterstock.com.

Cataloging-in-Publication Data

Names: Emminizer, Theresa.
Title: Ostrich: The largest bird / Theresa Emminizer.
Description: New York : PowerKids Press, 2020. | Series: Animal record breakers | Includes glossary and index.
Identifiers: ISBN 9781725308749 (pbk.) | ISBN 9781725308763 (library bound) | ISBN 9781725308756 (6 pack)
Subjects: LCSH: Ostriches–Juvenile literature.
Classification: LCC QL696.S9 E463 2020 | DDC 598.5'24–dc23

Manufactured in the United States of America

CPSIA Compliance Information: Batch #CWPK20. For Further Information contact Rosen Publishing, New York, New York at 1-800-237-9932.

CONTENTS

BIG BIRDS 4

UNIQUE CREATURES 6

IN THE WILD 8

FROM EGG TO ADULT..........................10

GROWING QUICKLY 12

LIFE IN THE HERD 14

SPECIAL DEFENSES 16

OSTRICHES IN TROUBLE......................18

CONSERVATION EFFORTS 20

OSTRICHES IN THE ECOSYSTEM 22

GLOSSARY 23

INDEX.. 24

WEBSITES................................... 24

BIG BIRDS

Ostriches are the biggest and heaviest birds in the world. They can reach heights of up to 9 feet (2.7 m) tall and weigh up to 350 pounds (158.7 kg).

Although they can't fly, ostriches can run at shocking speeds up to 43 miles (69 km) per hour and cover up to 16 feet (4.8 m) in a single bound. They're fast enough to outrun fearsome predators such as lions and cheetahs, and they're strong enough to kick them to death!

ANIMAL ACTION

If ostriches can't fly, then why do they have wings? When ostriches run, they stretch out their short wings to stay balanced.

Ostriches have the largest eyes of any land animal. Each eye measures almost 2 inches (5 cm) across.

UNIQUE CREATURES

Ostriches are unique, or one of a kind, animals. They are part of a group of animals called ratites, which are flightless birds. There are about 15 species, or kinds, of flightless birds that are in the same **order** as ostriches—struthioniformes. All have strong legs and small wings.

Ostriches are part of the Struthionidae family. Ostriches are the only living species in the *Struthio* **genus**. Even though each subspecies of ostriches looks different, they're all part of the same species—*Struthio camelus*.

OTHER STRUTHIONIFORMES

IN THE WILD

Ostriches can be found across Africa. They live in grassland, savannah, desert, and woodland **ecosystems**. Their predators include top hunters, such as lions and hyenas.

Ostriches are omnivores, which means they eat both plants and meat. Their diet is mostly made up of roots, leaves, and seeds. However, they'll also eat bugs, snakes, and lizards. They chase these animals, running in a zigzag pattern. Ostriches don't have teeth. Instead, they swallow small stones to help crush up their food.

ANIMAL ACTION

An ostrich's **intestines** are 46 feet (14 m) long. In addition to grinding their food with stones, they have three stomachs to help them digest, or break down, food.

If an ostrich can't find water, it can go several days without drinking.

FROM EGG TO ADULT

Ostrich eggs are the biggest eggs on Earth! Female ostriches lay up to 10 eggs at once. Measuring about 6 inches (15.2 cm) tall and 5 inches (12.7 cm) wide, ostrich eggs weigh about 3 pounds (1.4 kg).

Ostriches lay their eggs in shallow, or not deep, nests and work together to take care of them. The parents take turns lying on top of the eggs while they **incubate** for up to 46 days. Female ostriches watch the eggs during the day, and males watch them at night.

One ostrich egg weighs the same as 24 chicken eggs!

GROWING QUICKLY

When ostrich chicks hatch, or break out of their eggs, they're about the size of adult chickens. At first, they don't have long, soft feathers like adult ostriches do.

Ostrich chicks grow very quickly—almost a foot (30 cm) a month! By the time they're six months old they're almost fully grown. Ostriches reach adulthood when they're about four years old. At this point, they're ready to have chicks of their own. Ostriches can live to be 40 years old.

Ostrich chicks have short, stiff feathers.

LIFE IN THE HERD

Ostriches live in groups called herds. There are usually between 10 and 12 ostriches in a herd. A strong male and female pair lead each herd. Male ostriches fight with each other to become the herd leader.

Male ostriches have black and white feathers, while females and young ostriches have grayish-brown feathers. To attract, or draw in, females to have babies with, male ostriches do a special dance. They shake their wings and feathers and wag their heads and necks from side to side.

ANIMAL ACTION

Did you know that ostriches roar? When they feel **threatened**, male ostriches make loud, deep noises that sound like a lion roaring. Unhappy ostriches will also hiss.

Like chickens, female ostriches are called hens and males are called roosters. The lead female in a herd is called the "main hen."

SPECIAL DEFENSES

One reason ostriches live in herds is to help keep safe from predators. They also have other **defenses**. With their huge eyes, ostriches have very strong eyesight and can spot danger from far away. First, they'll try to run away. However, if they can't, they'll drop to the ground, stay very still, and try to **blend** in with the soil.

If attacked, ostriches use their strong legs and sharp talons, or claws, to defend themselves.

ANIMAL ACTION

It's a **myth** that ostriches bury their heads in the sand. Instead, they keep their head and neck flat against the ground to blend in with it.

Ostriches are the only birds that have two toes instead of three or four. This helps them run fast.

OSTRICHES IN TROUBLE

Ostriches face many threats. Apart from being hunted by top predators such as lions, humans also put these animals in danger. Roads, cities, and towns are cutting into the places ostriches live, shrinking their homes.

Ostriches are also hunted for their eggs, feathers, meat, and skin. Ostrich feathers are long and soft. Historically, they've been very popular in fashion. Since ancient times, ostrich plumes, or feathers, have been sought after as decorations for hats, helmets, and hairdos.

ANIMAL ACTION

During the 1700s, ostrich feather hats were so popular that ostrich feathers, along with gold and diamonds, became one of South Africa's top **exports**!

Ostrich farming began in 1838. If people hadn't begun farming ostriches instead of hunting them, it's possible that ostriches would have died out completely. Today, farmers still raise ostriches for their feathers, eggs, and meat.

CONSERVATION EFFORTS

Conservation is the effort to care for the natural world and protect it from harm. Today, ostriches aren't in danger of going extinct, or dying out completely. However, their numbers are dropping and efforts still need to be made to protect ostriches in the wild.

Ostriches have disappeared from certain parts of Africa, such as Niger, and efforts are being made to renew their populations, or numbers, there. This is accomplished through helping ostriches in those areas come together to have babies.

The North African ostrich is one ostrich subspecies whose numbers are dropping and needs to be protected.

OSTRICHES IN THE ECOSYSTEM

Ostriches are important members of their ecosystems. Ostriches share their ecosystem with other animals including zebras and giraffes. With their sharp eyesight, they help these animals by warning them if they spot danger, such as a lion or other predator.

By providing food for top predators, ostriches also play a key part in the food chain. By eating roots, leaves, and bugs, they keep their ecosystems healthy. These special animals are much more than just big birds!

GLOSSARY

blend: To look like the surroundings.

defense: A feature of a living thing that helps keep it safe.

ecosystem: A natural community of living and nonliving things.

export: Goods one country sells to another.

genus: The scientific name for a group of plants or animals that share most features.

incubate: To keep eggs warm.

intestines: Long tubes in the digestive system.

myth: A story that people make up to explain events.

order: In biology, a category to classify animals. It ranks above a family and below a class.

threatened: Likely to be harmed.

INDEX

C
chicks, 12
classification, 6
conservation, 20

D
defense, 16

E
ecosystem, 8, 22
eggs, 10
eyesight, 16, 22

F
farming, 18
feathers, 12, 14, 18
females, 10, 14
food, 8

H
herds, 14, 16

M
males, 10, 14

P
predators, 8, 22

R
ratites, 6

WEBSITES

Due to the changing nature of Internet links, PowerKids Press has developed an online list of websites related to the subject of this book. This site is updated regularly. Please use this link to access the list: www.powerkidslinks.com/arb/ostrich